Ánimo 2
Edexcel

Self Study Guide

Isabel Alonso de Sudea

OXFORD
UNIVERSITY PRESS

Great Clarendon Street, Oxford OX2 6DP

Oxford University Press is a department of the University of Oxford.
It furthers the University's objective of excellence in research, scholarship,
and education by publishing worldwide in

Oxford   New York

Auckland   Cape Town   Dar es Salaam   Hong Kong   Karachi
Kuala Lumpur   Madrid   Melbourne   Mexico City   Nairobi
New Delhi   Shanghai   Taipei   Toronto

With offices in

Argentina   Austria   Brazil   Chile   Czech Republic   France   Greece
Guatemala   Hungary   Italy   Japan   South Korea   Poland   Portugal
Singapore   Switzerland   Thailand   Turkey   Ukraine   Vietnam

Oxford is a registered trade mark of Oxford University Press
in the UK and in certain other countries

British Library Cataloguing in Publication Data

Data available

ISBN 978 019 915423 4

10 9 8 7 6 5 4 3 2 1

Typeset by PDQ Digital Media Solutions Ltd., Bungay, Suffolk

Printed in Great Britain by Ashford Colour Press Ltd.

Acknowledgements

The author and publisher would like to thank Imogen Fidler (editor) and
Ainara Solana (language consultant).

Contents

General exam tips   4
The grades at A level   5
How to revise   6

Speaking Tips   **8**
A2 Spanish: The Speaking Test   9

**Research, Understanding
and Written Response Unit**   14
Translation into Spanish   15
Essay writing   17

Grammar Summary   **24**
Nouns, determiners, adjectives, adverbs   25
Pronouns   26
Infinitives, the simple present and
present continuous tenses, impersonal
and third person verbs   27
Future and conditional tenses plus negatives   28
Past tenses – the preterite, imperfect
and past continuous   29
Compound tenses in the past   30
The subjunctive including
the imperative forms   31
More about the subjunctive   32
More complex tenses   33

Pronunciation   **34**

Vocabulary   **37**

Answers   **46**

Verb Table   **47**

Here's a reminder of the topics from the Edexcel A2 specification which you need to revise for the examination.

- Youth culture and concerns
- Lifestyle: health and fitness
- The world around us: travel, tourism, environmental issues and the Spanish-speaking world
- Education and employment
- Customs, traditions, beliefs and religions
- National and international events: past, present and future
- Literature and the arts

You will be taking two examinations:
(Remember that your AS grade represents 50% of your A Level.)

Unit 3: Understanding and Spoken Response in Spanish

The Speaking Test is worth 17.5% of your A Level.

The test lasts 11-13 minutes.

There is only one task: presenting any issue of your choice to the examiner in Spanish, taking a clear stance on it, discussing it with the examiner and moving on to discuss other issues.

Unit 4: Research, Understanding and Written Response in Spanish

This paper is worth 32.5% of your A Level.

The time allowed is 2 hours and 30 minutes.

There are three sections:

- Section A: Translating a short passage of English into Spanish
- Section B: Writing either a creative essay or a discursive essay of 240–270 words
- Section C: Writing a research-based essay of 240–270 words.

For the research-based essay you have to choose a topic from one of the following areas:

- Geographical area
- Historical study
- Aspects of modern society
- Literature and the arts

There is more information on the Unit 3 examination on page 8 and more information on the Unit 4 examination on page 14.

Pass grades for this examination range from A* and A down to E. The requirements are very similar to those for AS Level, but remember that this is in the context of the more demanding texts and tasks which you will meet at A2. Two new things which are expected are an ability to translate into Spanish accurately and an ability to cope with the unpredictable when you are talking to someone. Here's a reminder of the other expectations.

If you pass A Level Spanish with an A grade, it means you can:

▶ clearly understand the spoken language, including details and people's opinions.

▶ work out what someone is trying to say even if they don't spell it out in detail.

▶ clearly understand written texts, both the gist and the details.

▶ talk fluently, giving your opinions and justifying them, and using a good range of vocabulary and generally accurate pronunciation.

▶ organise your ideas and write them up well in Spanish.

▶ write using a wide range of vocabulary and grammatical structures without making many mistakes.

If you pass A Level Spanish with an E grade, it means you:

▶ show some understanding of spoken Spanish, even if you have difficulties when the language is complex and miss some of the details.

▶ can sometimes work out what someone is trying to say even if they don't give all the details.

▶ understand straightforward written texts, although you don't always understand more difficult writing.

▶ can talk in Spanish and convey basic information, perhaps a little hesitantly and relying on material you have learnt by heart. There is probably some English influence on your pronunciation.

▶ can convey information in writing, perhaps with some difficulty in organising your material and expressing it.

▶ use a range of vocabulary and structures, although quite often you make mistakes.

Preparing for the exams

You can see from these lists that when planning your revision there are really five areas you need to practise:

Speaking
Reading and research
Writing
Vocabulary
Grammar

There are tips on how to prepare each area on the page overleaf.

Speaking

▶ Take every opportunity to practise speaking Spanish – in lessons, with the language assistant, with a friend, with anyone you know who speaks Spanish.

▶ Keep researching the topic you have chosen for your oral exam, noting facts as well as useful vocabulary and expressions. Choose a topic you are interested in and then decide on a definite stance you want to take, arguing that some aspect is or is not a good thing, for example.

▶ Record some of your ideas, then listen to them to see which areas still need practice – perhaps fluency, pronunciation or good use of vocabulary and structures.

Reading and Research

▶ You need to read widely in order to research your chosen oral topic and also the material for your research-based essay.

▶ Once you have chosen an oral topic, read a good variety of texts in Spanish on it, looking for a suitable 'angle' to present to the examiner. When you are clear what you want to focus on, re-read everything of relevance, making notes on useful facts and ideas, but also listing vocabulary which will help you express them.

▶ Adopt a similar approach to the reading for your research-based essay, collecting relevant articles and making notes in sections. For example, if you are studying a book, you should make notes on each of the main characters, on the themes, perhaps a short biography of the author and so on.

▶ If you want to improve your general reading ability in Spanish, try magazines, material on the Internet which interests you or a 'dual-language' reading book, where you get the original Spanish on one page and an English translation on the opposite one. This is an excellent way to practise reading longer texts without losing heart!

Writing

▶ Write out the basic facts for each aspect of the cultural topics you have studied and learn them.

▶ Practise planning essay questions, both creative/discursive and research-based. Jot down ideas for each paragraph – in Spanish! – along with key vocabulary.

▶ Look carefully at marked work and identify what grammar errors you are making. Then check them in a grammar book and try some practice exercises.

▶ Make sure you are writing – and learning! – lists of key vocabulary for each aspect of your researched topic. In addition, learn a good range of 'essay phrases' for introducing ideas, giving opinions, summing up and so on.

Vocabulary

▸ Learn lists of words regularly and make time to go back over words you learned a week or two ago. Reinforcement makes them stick!

▸ Choose a system of recording new words which works for you. It could be paper lists, small sections on individual cards, recording the words and their English meanings on tape, making posters to stick on your bedroom wall ... what's important is that you are noting the words and going over them regularly!

▸ Go back over previous essays, highlighting good words and phrases and writing the English in the margin, then use this to test yourself. Words are often easier to learn in context.

Grammar

▸ Keep doing practice exercises in areas where you know you are weak.

▸ Use reading texts to practise thinking grammatically. For example, highlight a selection of adjectives, then write out the English for the phrases in which they appear. Test yourself by reproducing the Spanish phrases accurately, complete with all the correct agreements!

▸ Keep learning from your verb tables until you know all the forms of each tense of regular verbs and the most common irregular verbs. Test yourself using a die: 1 = *yo*, 2 = *tú*, 3 = *él / ella / usted*, 4 = *nosotros*, 5 = *vosotros*, 6 = *ellos / ellas / ustedes*. Use a verb list, choose an infinitive and a tense at random, throw the die and say the correct form of the verb. Practise until you can do it without hesitation.

Get the timing right!

Worthwhile revision is often a question of timing.

Some things need to be done as you go along and can't be left until the week before the exam. You should set regular time aside for learning and re-visiting your vocabulary lists and keep refining your knowledge of grammar. Regular speaking practice is a must – you can't make a lot of progress in the last few days!

So what can you do at the last minute? Keep your confidence up by going over vocabulary lists you have already revised, by reading through good essays you have written and perhaps writing plans for questions you haven't written up in full. In short, you should feel that you have already done all the important things and just need to keep things ticking over!

The Speaking Test: what you need to know

Your task is to present an issue and take a definite stance on it.

Timing

The test will last 11–13 minutes and be divided into three sections:

▶ 1 minute: you outline the issue you have chosen and explain your stance on it.

▶ 4 minutes: the examiner will challenge you to defend your point of view, asking you questions and taking the opposing viewpoint.

▶ 6–8 minutes: the examiner will then introduce a minimum of two other unprepared areas to discuss. These issues may or may not relate to your chosen issue, but it will be a general discussion in which you will not be required to show particular factual knowledge or knowledge of Spanish-language culture. The aim is to assess your speaking skills.

How the Speaking Test is marked

The test is marked out of 50, with marks given for four different aspects:

▶ **Response (20 marks)**
This rewards your ability to respond spontaneously and well to what you are asked, showing an impressive range of vocabulary and grammatical structures.

▶ **Quality of Response (7 marks)**
To do well here, you need to speak accurately, with very good pronunciation and intonation.

▶ **Reading and research (7 marks)**
You need to show evidence of in-depth research into your chosen topic and, when you are discussing the unprepared topics, of wide reading generally.

▶ **Comprehension and development (16 marks)**
You need to show a good understanding of what you are asked, even when the questions are complex or challenging. You need to be able to develop your answers, giving examples and evidence to back up your opinions.

What makes a good topic? Something you are interested in and have views about! It can be, but doesn't have to be, in a Spanish context, but you need to have read widely on the topic in Spanish in order to have the vocabulary to be able to discuss it well.

Here are three possible topics and stances:

▶ Centrales nucleares: la única solución para las necesidades energéticas del futuro.

▶ El bachillerato: más diverso, más detallado y más interesante que el A Level.

▶ Las películas de Almodóvar siempre estarán de moda.

Planning your presentation

You have only one minute in which to introduce your topic and present the stance you want to take on it, so you need to be very clear about what you are trying to say. You will probably want to write your presentation out and then learn it and should use no more than 150–170 words in total. Time it to make sure it lasts about a minute. You need to state what your topic is, explain the stance you want to take on it and give some general reasons. Remember that the examiner will come back to the points you make and challenge you on them, so make sure you have your justifications ready!

Useful phrases for this section include:

He escogido / decidido hablar sobre ... porque ...
Me parece que / Estoy convencido de que ...
En mi opinión ...
Lo digo por / Hay varias razones, por ejemplo ...
¿Por qué? Pues simplemente porque ...

Of course research and a good knowledge of your topic are vital. There isn't room to show off everything you know in the initial presentation, but you should mention there the things you will be happy to come back to. For each aspect you mention, you need to prepare a set of well-organised notes. Write the key facts for each and learn them: you won't be asked to recite them, but you will be able to slip them in as examples to illustrate the points you are making. Knowing your material really well will give you the confidence to speak fluently.

You know that the examiner is going to challenge your views. Try to predict what s/he might ask and then decide what you are going to say in response. There is more information on this aspect on page 10.

Once everything is planned, you just need to practise! Make a note of the questions you are asked in practice sessions with your teacher or the assistant, so that you gradually build up a list of things you can answer well. You can practise on your own by using these questions and recording your responses. Listen to them with the Edexcel mark scheme in front of you and analyse how you are doing.

Defending your case

The examiner will challenge your views. This is **not** an exercise which requires you to balance both sides of an argument. You must stick to your initial argument and defend it! You need to have two things ready:

▸ a list of reasons why you think the way you do

▸ an idea of all the arguments the examiner might use to argue against you and – this is important! – points you can make against each of them.

Imagine you have decided to argue in favour of renewable sources of energy. Notes on your arguments might include:

▸ una solución que nos permita utilizar menos recursos no renovables y de esta forma proteger el planeta.

▸ la solución nuclear es peligrosa – hay demasiado riesgo de accidentes o atentados terroristas, está el problema de los desechos, la dificultad de desmantelar las centrales, etc.

▸ ya es una solución y dadas las investigaciones que se están llevando a cabo hoy en día podemos intuir que ofrecerá más posibilidades en el futuro.

The examiner might use some of the following arguments. Decide what you would say to counter each one, then compare your ideas with those printed upside down below.

1 ¿Usted cree que es realista querer producir toda la energía que necesitaremos en el futuro mediante recursos renovables?

2 ¡Pero la energía eólica no podrá ser empleada jamás para el transporte!

3 Las necesidades energéticas no cesan de aumentar. ¿Usted cree que podemos depender de los recursos renovables para proporcionarnos la energía necesaria en todo momento?

1 Por el momento no me parece del todo realista pero hay que seguir investigando y con los nuevos métodos que descubramos creo que será posible en el futuro. Se han hecho bastantes progresos durante los últimos 20 años.

2 Nunca se sabe. Pero lo cierto es que ya hay coches eléctricos. Además, si se consigue producir más energía hidroeléctrica creo que existirán otras opciones viables.

3 En este caso creo que lo que debe cambiar es nuestro comportamiento. Desperdiciamos mucha energía y deberíamos aprender a limitarnos. Algunas maneras de ahorrar energía son, por ejemplo, viajar menos, comprar productos locales y otras tan fáciles como bajar la temperatura de la calefacción o sacar la ropa al jardín en vez de usar la secadora de ropa.

Read and listen to this student defending his argument. His topic is social integration and he has taken the stance that tolerance and respect for the individual are the best way to ensure greater social integration. This is the section where the examiner begins to challenge his views (track 2).

Las divisiones sociales siempre han existido y siempre existirán ¿verdad?

Claro que existen diferencias culturales y de costumbres. Siempre ha habido diferentes lenguas, idiomas y creencias, pero una sociedad civilizada fomenta la tolerancia y el respeto y es precisamente esto lo que sirve para consolidar y fortalecer la cohesión social. Tenemos muchos ejemplos de ello. Son los políticos los que muchas veces no quieren comprender o prefieren dividir a la gente por sus ansias de poder y riqueza.

No se puede negar que muchas veces son las diferencias de riqueza las que dividen a la sociedad y causan problemas.

No cabe duda y es evidente en todas las sociedades del mundo, pero esto no quiere decir que sea una barrera a la integración. Al contrario, los que tienen más tienen una responsabilidad hacia los que tienen menos. Lo que pasa con el sistema de comercio libre es que la avaricia y el egoísmo prevalecen. Los sistemas de impuestos son un ejemplo que demuestra hasta qué punto queremos ayudar a los menos favorecidos de nuestra sociedad.

¿Qué me dice de los grupos que no se quieren integrar en la sociedad y se automarginan?

No creo que tenga usted razón cuando dice que no quieren integrarse. Lo que pasa es que se sienten marginados y rechazados porque saben que no van a ser aceptados o porque perciben actitudes xenófobas producto de discursos populistas. A veces se juntan por miedo a lo desconocido pero cuando llegan a familiarizarse con la comunidad donde viven las cosas cambian para bien.

Es un poco ingenuo pensar que la víctima de un crimen vaya a abrazar a un chaval que le ha robado o hasta causado daño físico ¿no le parece?

Me parece que la prensa popular es la responsable de ciertos prejuicios que tenemos respecto a este tema. Hay que tener en cuenta que el comportamiento antisocial es a menudo el producto de las diferencias sociales. A mi modo de ver siempre es mucho mejor tratar de reintegrar a una persona y reeducarla para que pueda participar en la sociedad de una manera positiva. Los castigos sólo sirven para que siga siendo una fuente de conflicto en la sociedad en que vive.

Bueno ahora me gustaría saber por qué ...

Learn some useful phrases for disagreeing (politely!) with the examiner. Examples include:

No creo; al contrario; yo creo que ...
No estoy de acuerdo con usted en absoluto, porque ...
En mi opinión usted no tiene razón / usted se equivoca porque ...
Pues, yo diría que ...
Posiblemente que sí, pero no hay que olvidarse de que ...

The last 6–8 minutes of the Speaking Test will be a spontaneous discussion on at least two unprepared areas. These may – or may not! – relate to the topic you chose to talk about. It's worth making a list of possible areas which lead on from your topic, because the examiner may well start with one of those. Advice on this is given below. See page 13 for information about other topics which might come up in this section.

For example, if your topic was tourism and you argued that tourism is always bad for the environment, the examiner might decide to move onto other environmental issues or to something related to travel and tourism. Possible questions include:

▶ ¿Qué otros aspectos del medio ambiente le interesan?

▶ ¿Qué hace usted para proteger el medio ambiente?

▶ ¿Cree usted que se habla demasiado sobre el medio ambiente hoy día?

▶ ¿Cuáles son las ventajas del turismo para una región?

▶ ¿Qué regiones de España conoce usted?

▶ ¿Le gusta ser turista o prefiere vivir más tiempo en un país extranjero?

▶ ¿Piensa viajar en el futuro? ¿Por qué (no)?

Look at these possible topics and stances and for each one think up three questions the examiner might ask in order to move the conversation on to a different topic. Then compare your answers with those printed upside down below.

1 Se habla demasiado sobre la comida sana. Si se hace suficiente deporte se puede comer de todo.

2 La cultura es sólo para la gente mayor y no tiene nada que ver con los jóvenes.

3 Cinco años en el mismo empleo es demasiado tiempo.

: Do the same for your own topic. Write a list of possible opening
: questions on related topics and practise answering them. You can't
: guarantee they will come up, but there's a reasonable chance!

3
En España no trabajan horas fijas. ¿Le parece bueno?
¿Cuáles son las razones para el desempleo entre los 18 y los 25 años?
¿Cómo sería para usted el empleo ideal?

2
¿Cómo le gustaría pasar su jubilación?
¿Qué hay que hacer para animar a los músicos jóvenes?
¿Quién es su autor preferido y por qué?

1
¿Aquí en su colegio se hace suficiente deporte?
¿Usted cree que los deportistas famosos ganan demasiado dinero?
¿Qué piensa usted que perjudica más a la salud – el alcohol o el tabaco?

Other topics which could crop up in the last part of the speaking test are listed in the specification. Here are a few sample questions as examples of what you might be asked. You can listen to students answering these similar questions on the CD (track 3) and find a transcript in a Microsoft Word® document on the CD.

Youth culture and concerns

▶ ¿Cuáles son las características de la cultura juvenil de hoy día?

▶ Deme algunos ejemplos de personas que sirvan de modelo para los jóvenes.

▶ ¿Cuáles son las causas principales de la delincuencia juvenil?

Lifestyle: health and fitness

▶ ¿Cree usted que se habla demasiado sobre la salud hoy en día?

▶ ¿Qué aspecto de la salud de los jóvenes le preocupa más?

▶ ¿Se puede decir que nuestra sociedad es menos sana que nunca?

The world around us: travel, tourism, environmental issues and the Spanish-speaking world

▶ ¿Usted opina que se aprende viajando?

▶ ¿Usted cree que el turismo tiene más inconvenientes que ventajas?

▶ ¿Qué hay que hacer para vivir realizando el mínimo gasto energético?

▶ ¿Qué aspecto de la contaminación le preocupa más?

Education and employment

▶ ¿Cómo juzga usted la educación que ha recibido?

▶ ¿Debemos animar a los jóvenes a hacer estudios superiores?

▶ ¿Cuáles son las consecuencias del desempleo en la sociedad en general?

Customs, traditions, beliefs and religions

▶ ¿Qué tradiciones piensa usted que son importantes?

▶ ¿Qué importancia tiene la fe en la sociedad actual?

National and international events: past, present and future

▶ ¿Qué se puede aprender estudiando historia?

▶ ¿Vale la pena votar?

▶ ¿Habrá siempre guerras?

Literature and the arts

▶ Hable sobre una obra literaria o película que le haya afectado profundamente.

▶ ¿Si tuviera que organizar una feria cultural, cuáles serían sus metas principales?

This unit takes 2 hours and 30 minutes.

There are three sections and they will all be linked to the topic list which you can find on page 4.

You can plan your time as you wish, but it might be best to allow at least an hour for each of the two essays, which would leave up to half an hour to spend on Section A.

Section A (10 marks)

A short passage of about 80 words of English which you have to translate into Spanish.

Section B (45 marks)

Either: a discursive essay of between 240 and 270 words.

This type of essay requires you to argue a point, balance the pros and cons of an argument or give your opinion on a topic and justify it.

Or: a creative essay of between 240 and 270 words.

You may be asked to write the story behind a photograph or document, to continue a story opening which you are given or to produce some other form of imaginary writing.

Section C (45 marks)

A research-based essay of between 240 and 270 words. There will be one question on each of the research-based topic areas:

▸ Geographical area
▸ Historical study
▸ Aspects of modern society
▸ Literature and the arts

The key ways to prepare are by:
▸ doing plenty of practice of translation into Spanish, revising vocabulary and grammar points as you go.
▸ practising writing creative or discursive essays (240–270 words) on each of the general topic areas listed on page 4.
▸ choosing a research topic which really interests you, discussing the areas you plan to focus on with your teacher and researching it, making careful notes on the different aspects as you go. Then writing practice essays (240–270 words).
▸ working through the exam-type questions and tips on the following pages.

Translation task 1

Traduce las frases siguientes al español.

a) After months of very little rain Catalonia has had to ask Madrid for help.

b) However, it's doubtful they will be able to resolve the problem quickly.

c) The country is trying to deal with the worst drought in forty years.

d) Catalonia, in the north-east, has been severely affected.

e) Authorities in Barcelona are going to fine people for watering the garden.

f) No one is allowed to fill a swimming pool of more than 300 square metres.

g) Fountains have been emptied and beach showers turned off.

Think grammatically! Which sentence or sentences require you to use each of the following? Work it out, then check the answers, which are printed upside down.

 i the present continuous tense

 ii a verb which is followed by 'por'

 iii a phrase followed by the subjunctive

 iv an infinitive where English uses the '-ing' form of the verb

 v a negative construction

 vi a superlative

 vii a verb in the passive

 viii a verb in the perfect tense

 ix a definite article where you don't need one in English

 i c; ii c, e; iii b; iv e; v f; vi c; vii g; viii a, d and g; ix e

---

Check the grammar of your finished translations very carefully. Is every verb in the correct tense and does it agree with its subject? Does every adjective agree with the noun it describes?

Translation task 2

Translate into Spanish:

In this day and age we are all very aware of the positive aspects of the Internet and there are very few of us who do not take advantage of them. No one doubts that it is a very powerful tool which brings huge benefits to its users. Besides, every day prices are falling so that it is becoming more and more accessible for a greater number of people.

However, at the same time it is important to recognise that the Internet is a public forum and therefore open to abuse. As a consequence we all need to take care about what kind of information we give out over the Internet, but most of all we should insist that the government provide regulations to combat cyber crime and help to protect younger users.

Always try to spot the "grammar tricks" the examiner has planted in the English passage. To translate the first paragraph well, you need to remember that even though the phrase 'no one doubts' sounds quite positive in English it requires the subjunctive in Spanish. Always take care over idiomatic translations such as 'to take advantage of' and 'more and more'.

Be especially careful over the spelling of words which are similar to, but not quite the same as, their English equivalents. In this passage, words like this include the translations of 'accessible', 'recognise', 'consequence' and 'information'.

When checking your translation, look especially at the verb forms. Have you used the correct form of the verb to translate 'very few of us' and 'it is becoming' in the first paragraph? Have you correctly translated the phrase 'we all need to take care' in the second paragraph and have you remembered that you need to put not only 'provide' in the final sentence into the subjunctive after the verb 'insist', but also the second verb 'help'?

Good essay writing is really the key to this paper, as it is worth 90% of the marks! Whichever sort of essay you are writing, there are three vital stages: planning, writing and checking, and you need to find time for all three, even under exam conditions.

Planning

Don't rush this stage. Five to ten minutes thinking about the question, deciding on your argument and dividing it into paragraphs, jotting down the facts you want to use and thinking out a good introduction and conclusion is time very well spent. Keep referring to the title to make sure every paragraph is relevant to the question. You might also note vocabulary and phrases you want to use in each paragraph. Then, when everything is in order, start writing, and make sure you stick to the plan!

Writing

Work through your notes for each paragraph. Write them up using a variety of sentence lengths, interesting vocabulary and a range of grammatical constructions. Be especially careful about the links between the paragraphs, so the examiner can follow the argument easily. See the ideas on page 23.

Checking

Read your essay through once to check the flow of ideas and make sure each sentence makes sense. Then do a more detailed check, looking especially for these common errors:

▸ verbs which don't agree with their subject or are in the wrong tense

▸ adjectives which don't agree with the noun they describe

▸ phrases which are not idiomatic and don't sound Spanish

▸ misspellings, especially of words similar to, but not the same as, English

▸ missing accents

It's also useful to practise planning essays, even if you don't write them up in full. Writing well-thought-out plans for possible essay titles is excellent revision in itself, and gives you some material to look over in the last revision periods before the exam.

Make some useful revision notes by copying out sentences from your essays which had mistakes in them and then putting in the corrections in a different colour. Doing this will remind you of errors you have made and – even more importantly – of how to correct them!

Obviously, your essay needs a beginning, a middle and an end, but there are different ways to plan it. Here are a few possibilities:

For and against

This is the classic 'balanced argument' technique where you write one or two paragraphs in favour of something, then one or two more against it and then conclude with your personal opinion.

Tennis match

This is another useful way to structure an essay in which you want to put forward both sides of an argument. Each paragraph is used to put forward a point from one side of the argument, then give the reasons against it. It is useful if you want to put one side of the argument over strongly; each paragraph gives a reason for your argument, then explains why those opposed to it are wrong. The essay then needs to end with a strong conclusion.

Chronological

A chronological approach is suitable for certain types of question. An essay about plot development in a film or a novel can follow this pattern, as long as you are careful not to lapse into just re-telling the story. You may want to describe a character at the beginning of the story, refer to events which happen and their effect on him or her and then conclude by saying how he or she has changed. It could also be a useful approach for an essay about, say, the impact of tourism on a particular region, if you wanted to explain how the industry has developed over time.

Build the argument

Some essays practically plan themselves! If you want to write about the way cinematic techniques contribute to plot development in a film, you may decide that the relevant points are sound, lighting, the use of flashbacks and the range of camera angles used. So it makes sense to devote one paragraph to each of these, making each point clear by giving examples and then saying what the effect of each is. Top and tail this with an introduction and conclusion (see page 19) and you have a perfect plan!

Make a point of using different styles of essay plan in the practice essays you write so you become familiar with the possibilities and see what works best in each particular set of circumstances.

The Beginning

Your introduction needs to set the scene. It should pose the question you will be answering, but not give away your conclusion. Look at these notes for possible introductions for particular titles.

Analiza el tema principal de la película _Mar Adentro_.

Para mí el tema más importante de esta película es el del derecho a la muerte asistida. La lucha personal del tetrapléjico Ramón Sampedro (papel desempeñado por Javier Bardem) dio nueva vida al debate sobre la eutanasia y el derecho a poder elegir una muerte digna. Creo que tuvo mucho coraje Alejandro Amenábar, el director, cuando decidió profundizar en este tema y enfrentarse a la iglesia católica que, como era de esperar, ha lanzado una crítica feroz contra la película.

Sin el turismo, la comunidad valenciana no sería una región tan desarrollada. Analiza y comenta esta declaración.

Sin lugar a dudas es una región que atrae mucho turismo, tanto nacional como extranjero. En primer lugar por el mar y la costa. Los turistas vienen en busca de sol, playa y descanso; los españoles a pueblos típicos como Moraira, y los extranjeros – muchos alemanes – a Calpe.

Pero ¿es verdad que depende totalmente del turismo? Voy a explicar la importancia que tiene el turismo para Valencia analizando a la vez la relación de interdependencia con otras industrias.

The Middle

Stick to the paragraph plan you have worked out. Make it easy for the examiner to follow your argument by 'signposting' it, giving an indication at the beginning of each new paragraph as to what point you are going to make and how it follows on from the previous paragraph. Is it another point in the same argument or does it contradict your previous point?

Adding a new argument:

Hay que mencionar también que ...
Además debo decir que ...
Tampoco hay que olvidar que ...
Más importante aún es ...
Al mismo tiempo ...

Contradicting your previous point:

En cambio ...
Por el contrario ...
Sin embargo no todo el mundo está de acuerdo. Hay ciertas personas que creen que ...
Quizás la verdad es más compleja, ...
¿Eso es verdad? No necesariamente: citemos por ejemplo ...

The End

The conclusion is the place to answer the question and to give your personal viewpoint, which should arise logically out of the arguments you have put forward.

Useful phrases include:

Llego entonces a la conclusión de que ...
Después de considerarlo a fondo pienso que ...
Todo lo cual sirve para demostrar que ...
A fin de cuentas creo que ...

What you have to do

A stimulus is provided and you are asked to write an imaginative response to it. The stimulus could be a photo or cartoon, for which you are asked to imagine how the situation came about or perhaps predict what might happen next. The stimulus could also be a text, perhaps a diary extract or other piece of writing which you are asked to respond to or continue in your own words.

Typical questions

1 Cuenta la historia de estos dos jóvenes.

2 Continúa esta historia utilizando el tiempo pasado.
La primera vez que vi a Miguel parecía bastante confuso. Con la camisa un poco rota y la cara manchada se acercó a mí con una expresión perpleja. Yo, ...

3 Escribe un artículo para este titular:

Dos jóvenes ganan el viaje de sus sueños

Some teachers don't prepare their classes for this type of essay, concentrating instead on practising discursive essays. If that's the case, don't try this out in the exam! You need to have had several practice essays marked so that you can see exactly what the requirements are.

How the essay is marked

There are 45 marks in total, allocated as follows:

Range and application of language: 10 marks
i.e. a good range of vocabulary and complex structures, well handled.

Accuracy: 5 marks

Understanding and response: 15 marks
i.e. a good understanding of the question and an imaginative response to it.

Organisation and development: 15 marks
i.e. a clear, well-planned piece which is easy to follow and where the ideas are developed.

What you have to do

A discursive essay requires you to organise ideas and arguments and build a well-structured answer to a question on a general issue. The information on essay structures on pages 17 and 18 is particularly relevant here.

Remember that the essay questions will all relate to the general topic areas from the specification, so learning vocabulary for each one will be really useful, as will revising the essays you have written on these topics during the year. Look through your textbook for ideas for other questions on each topic and write plans for them – re-reading them will be useful last-minute revision.

Typical questions

1 La impresión que dan la mayoría de los jóvenes hoy en día no es muy buena. ¿Estás de acuerdo?

2 ¿Cree usted que la mayoría de la gente no hace deporte para divertirse sino por salud?

3 ¿Por qué seguir viajando en esta época de crisis medioambiental a nivel planetario?

4 ¿Cuáles deberían ser los objetivos de la enseñanza secundaria?

5 ¿Eres de la opinión que en el mundo moderno ya no necesitamos un dios?

6 ¿Crees que para ser 'culto' hay que estar al tanto de los sucesos nacionales e internacionales?

7 ¿Consideras que la literatura está pasada de moda en el mundo actual?

It's important to come up with a wide-ranging answer to the question and to devise separate paragraphs to make your various points. For question 3, for example, you might write first on the merits of travel, and then on how to limit the environmental effects of your journeys, before concluding that travel can be useful for learning more about the earth we are trying to protect.

How the essay is marked

There are 45 marks in total.

Three sections are exactly the same as for the creative essay, so check the information on page 20: range and application of language (10 marks), accuracy (5 marks) and organisation and development (15 marks).

The remaining 15 marks are for understanding and response, which for the discursive essay means that you have fully understood all the implications of the question and answered it well.

What you have to do

You need to choose a topic from one of the four topic areas listed below and conduct your own research so that you can answer an essay question on it. The questions require you to present relevant aspects of your research and convey your own views and opinions on the topic. The questions will all require answers which analyse and evaluate what you have found out, rather than just stating the facts.

Here are ideas for the type of research areas which would be required for each type of topic:

Geographical area (eg a region or a city)

Key people and events; issues which affect the area, such as demographic, environmental, economic, social and political factors.

Historical study

A specific period of history relevant to Spain or a Spanish-speaking country, including key people, events and issues.

Aspects of modern Spanish-speaking society

Key current and recent* events; social, political and cultural issues.
*recent means 21st or late 20th century.

Literature and the arts

A study of a text, play or film, including its characters, key themes, social and cultural setting and style or techniques.

Conducting research

You need to consult a wide range of source material on the topic you have chosen, because this will give you a broad spectrum of views and lots of useful vocabulary ideas.
Of course the Internet will provide a lot of material, but other sources likely to be relevant to each topic area include the following:

Geographical area (eg a region or a city)

Material from the relevant tourist board, personal experiences if you have visited the area, interviews with those who know it well.

Historical study

History textbooks, encylopaedias.

Aspects of modern Spanish-speaking society

Newspapers and magazines, online news services, interviews with relevant people, TV and radio programmes.

Literature and the arts

The actual text or film; books or films by the same author or director; critical material; the arts sections of newspapers or websites.

Keep copies or recordings of all the source material you use, so that you can refer to it as you work on your revision notes. When you make notes, list the source of all the facts so that you can find them again if you want to check them or find out more.

Here are some typical questions.

Geographical area

▶ Considera los factores geográficos de la región o del país que has estudiado y evalúa su importancia.

▶ Analiza la influencia de los factores económicos en la región o país que has estudiado.

Historical study

▶ Analiza las causas y los efectos de un suceso importante del período que has estudiado.

▶ Elige a un personaje clave del período que has estudiado. ¿Qué crees que nos puede enseñar?

Aspects of modern Spanish-speaking society

▶ ¿Qué aspecto de la sociedad hispanoparlante contemporánea le fascina más? ¿Por qué?

▶ Escoge un aspecto de la sociedad hispanoparlante contemporánea. ¿Qué te parece la situación actual y cómo ves el futuro?

Literature and the arts

▶ ¿Admiras el estilo del autor / guionista que has estudiado? ¿Por qué (no)?

▶ Compara y contrasta a dos personajes del libro / de la película que has estudiado.

It's good essay style to weave facts and opinions together, as in this extract on the effects of the Civil War as they are felt today:

Sí, creo que sí, sobre todo en las personas de la tercera edad. Los jóvenes sólo tienen los recuerdos de sus abuelos, si es que siguen con vida. Durante la dictadura de Franco no se hablaba de las atrocidades y las consecuencias de la guerra, pero desde la transición a la democracia en 1975 y a medida que la fecha se ha ido alejando la gente ha desarrollado más coraje para enfrentarse a su historia. Recientemente la nueva ley de la memoria histórica ha abierto viejas controversias y mucha gente teme las consecuencias.

The student who wrote this is evaluating one of the effects of this period of history on modern-day Spain, but s/he has also slipped several facts into the paragraph: the existence of the dictatorship and Franco, the date of the beginning of the period of transition and the fact that there is a new law which is reviewing 'historical memory' and opening old wounds.

The marks for this question are awarded as follows:

Reading, research and understanding: 30 marks
i.e. clear evidence of extensive, in-depth reading and research.

Organisation and development: 9 marks
i.e. organising your material effectively into a well-planned essay.

Quality of language: 6 marks
i.e. fluent and varied language showing a wide vocabulary and a command of a good range of complex structures as well as a high level of grammatical accuracy.

Grammar Summary

All the grammar you learned for AS is still needed and there are some extra points for A2. Pages 25-31 revise AS grammar, reminding you what you should know and giving you phrases and sentences to translate into Spanish for practice. Pages 32-33 revise the points you will be learning on the A2 course, also practised through sentences to translate.

Grammar is even more important at A2 than it was at AS. So, what can you do to make sure you really do know your stuff?

Pay attention when grammar is explained! If you learn the rules and their exceptions and do some practice exercises, you will be surprised how much of it will stick.

Accept that there is quite a lot of detail to master and be prepared to go over things regularly. Re-read your grammar notes, re-do practice exercises, ask questions if you come across things you don't fully understand.

Be pro-active. Go through marked written work, looking carefully at the things which have been corrected. Decide which ones are 'silly mistakes' caused by forgetting things which you know well, and make a list of them so you can try to avoid them in the future. Then look for errors where you are not quite sure what is wrong. Ask, if necessary, then look that grammar point up in the grammar section of your textbook and in the relevant section of the grammar workbook. Keep practising and asking questions until you do understand it. When you understand it, review it by writing grammar notes on it in your own words, adding examples.

Make a list of example sentences from your written work which use some of the more complex grammar points well. Learn them, and use them as models for other sentences with different vocabulary but using the same basic structure. Make a point of including a good variety of grammatical structures in the practice essays you write.

Work through the exercises on the following pages. If there are practice sentences you find hard to translate, learn the correct version from the answer section by heart.

Revision of AS Grammar: nouns, determiners, adjectives, adverbs

Check the grammar section of Ánimo 2 and/or the Grammar Workbook if you need to know more about any of these areas:

▸ typical masculine endings for nouns, such as *-o, -e, -l, -r, -u, -y* and exceptions

▸ typical feminine endings for nouns, such as *-a, -ión, -ad, -ed* and exceptions

▸ forming plural nouns and adjectives; vowel + *s*; consonant + *es*; *z* —▸ *ces*

▸ when to use and when not to use the definite and indefinite articles

▸ how and when to shorten adjectives like *grande* —▸ *gran*; *bueno* —▸ *buen* etc.

▸ how the position of an adjective can change its meaning: *un gran hombre / un hombre grande*

▸ forming possessive adjectives like *mi, tu, su, nuestro/a/os/as; vuestro/a/os/as; sus*

▸ forming adverbs using the feminine form of the adjective plus *-mente* and irregular adverbs like *bien* and *mal.*

▸ using *más, menos* and *tan / como* to form comparisons and *el más* or *el menos* to form superlatives

▸ using irregular comparisons like *mejor / peor / menor / mayor* or irregular superlatives like *el mejor / el peor*

Translate into Spanish:

1 Milk is healthier than coffee.

2 Salt is not good for you either.

3 You should drink water every day.

4 Lights in town are brighter than they used to be.

5 My mother is a nurse and my bother is a journalist.

6 Her dream is to be a great tennis player.

7 Spanish wine is just as good as French wine.

8 Our house uses less energy now than before.

9 That is the worst picture you have painted.

10 You are the third man to ask me that question.

1 La leche es más saludable que el café.

2 La sal tampoco es buena.

3 Deberías beber agua todos los días.

4 Las luces de la ciudad son más brillantes que antes.

5 Mi madre es enfermera y mi hermano es periodista.

6 Su sueño es ser un gran tenista.

7 El vino español es tan bueno como el vino francés.

8 Nuestra casa usa menos energía ahora que antes.

9 Ese es el peor cuadro que has pintado.

10 Usted es el tercer hombre que me ha hecho esa pregunta.

Grammar Summary

Revision of AS Grammar: pronouns

Check the grammar section of Ánimo 2 and/or the Grammar Workbook if you need to know more about any of these areas:

▶ personal pronouns: *tú / vosotros; usted / ustedes*

▶ direct object pronouns: *me, te, lo, la, nos, os, los, las*

▶ indirect object pronouns: *me, te, le, nos, os, les*

▶ emphatic pronouns, used after prepositions: *para mi, ti, él, ella, nosotros, vosotros, ellos, ellas*

▶ reflexive pronouns, used with reflexive verbs: *me, te, se, nos, os, se*

▶ the position of pronouns in a sentence, especially when there is more than one: *me los dio; dámelos ahora; ¿Cuándo vas a levantarte? Ya se ha levantado.*

▶ when two third person object pronouns come together change the first one to *se*

▶ the relative pronoun *que*, which you can never leave out as you can in English

▶ other relative pronouns: *de quien / quienes; el que / el cual; donde*

▶ possessive pronouns: *el mío / la mía / los míos / las mías* etc.; *el tuyo, el suyo, el nuestro, el vuestro, los suyos,* which agree in gender and number with the noun they modify

▶ demonstrative adjectives and pronouns: *este / esta / estos / estas*

▶ indefinite pronouns and adjectives: *alguno (algún) / alguna / algunos / algunas*

Translate into Spanish

1 Explain to me what you want from me.

2 Which of these two presents do you prefer?

3 These shirts are the best. I don't like those.

4 Someone loves you but I'm not sure who!

5 That's her book so give it to her now please.

6 Here's some chocolate. Eat it all up – it won't make you fat.

7 These are my glasses. Where are yours?

8 I prefer to sit by the fire in winter. What about you?

9 Whose is this CD? Is it hers or his?

10 Neither. I think it must be ours.

1 Explícame lo que quieres de mí.

2 ¿Cuál de estos dos regalos prefieres?

3 Estas camisas son las mejores. No me gustan aquéllas.

4 Alguien te quiere pero no estoy seguro de quién!

5 Ése es su libro, así que dáselo ahora, por favor.

6 Aquí tienes chocolate. Cómetelo todo – no te engordará.

7 Estas son mis gafas. ¿Dónde están las tuyas?

8 Prefiero sentarme al lado de la chimenea en invierno. ¿Y tú?

9 ¿De quién es este CD? ¿Es de ella o de él?

10 Ninguno de los dos. Creo que debe de ser nuestro.

Revision of AS Grammar: infinitives, the simple present and present continuous tenses, impersonal and third person verbs

• •
Check the grammar section of Ánimo 2 and/or the Grammar Workbook if you need to know more about any of these areas:
• •

▶ the use of the infinitive as a noun, in instructions or in two-verb constructions e.g. *sonreír es bueno; no pisar el cesped; ¿Me permite fumar? hacer venir*

▶ the infinitive as used after verbs followed by the prepositions *a* and *de*, such as *ayudar a, tratar de, volver a, acabar de*

▶ the present tense of regular and radical changing verbs, such as *hablar, comer, vivir; jugar (ue), empezar (ie), dormir (ue), pedir (i)* and where the spelling changes occur

▶ the present tense of the modal verbs *querer, deber* and *poder*

▶ the present tense of irregular verbs such as *ir, tener, hacer*, and the different usages of *ser* and *estar* plus many less common irregular verbs

▶ the present participle and the present continuous; *-ando; -iendo; estoy leyendo; está durmiendo*

▶ the use of the present tense with *desde (hace)*

▶ the passive form of the present tense in sentences like *su beca es pagada por el gobierno*

▶ the use of *gustar* and other third person and impersonal verbs; *me interesa; no se puede entrar*

Translate into Spanish

1 I always make it clear that I don't like racism.

2 We try to help people to understand the issues.

3 Tolerance plays an important part in social integration.

4 Children play together without a problem.

5 We must work hard to prevent local crime.

6 Why are such stupid laws allowed to be passed?

7 He has been organising political campaigns for years.

8 It's good to take part in charity walks.

9 They are looking for other ways to support the cause.

10 I am delighted to work for this charity.

10 Me encanta trabajar para esta ONG.

9 Están buscando otras maneras de apoyar la causa.

8 Es bueno participar en caminatas benéficas.

7 Hace años que organiza campañas políticas.

6 ¿Por qué se permite que se aprueben leyes tan estúpidas?

5 Debemos trabajar duro para prevenir el crimen local.

4 Los niños juegan juntos sin problema.

3 La tolerancia desempeña un papel importante en la cohesión social.

2 Tratamos de ayudar a la gente a comprender los asuntos.

1 Siempre dejo claro que no me gusta el racismo.

Revision of AS Grammar: future and conditional tenses plus negatives

Check the grammar section of Ánimo 2 and/or the Grammar Workbook if you need to know more about any of these areas:

▸ using the present tense to refer to things which are going to happen soon, especially if a future time is mentioned: *voy a casa de mi amiga esta noche; ¿por qué no vemos este programa mañana?*

▸ using *ir* + infinitive to say what is going to happen in the near future: *voy a llegar tarde esta noche; vamos a bailar el sábado por la noche*

▸ using *me gustaría; tengo la intención de; pienso* etc. + an infinitive to refer to future plans which are not certain: *me gustaría viajar por el mundo algún día; ¿Tú piensas continuar tus estudios en la Universidad?*

▸ forming the future tense of regular verbs by adding *-é, -ás, -á, -emos, -éis, -án* to the infinitive form: *estudiaré, comeremos, vivirán*

▸ forming the future tense of irregular verbs: *iré, haremos, dirán*

▸ forming the conditional tense using the future stem and imperfect endings *-ía, -ías, -ía, -íamos, -íais, ían* and using it to refer to what would happen or what you would do: *yo que tú iría en barco; sería difícil hacerlo en seguida; dijo que lo haría*

▸ using negative words before and after the verb: *nada, nadie, nunca, tampoco, ni ... ni*

Translate into Spanish

1 Spain intends to stay in the European Union for now.

2 Soon we will all be buying things online.

3 It would be a good idea to start learning more about computing now.

4 If I were you I would not allow my child free access to such websites.

5 Medical advances will help cure diseases in the developing world.

6 Why don't we think about the harm we are going to cause to the planet?

7 We would all like to have a perfect world.

8 It could be easy but no one is willing to make the effort.

9 It would be great if GM crops could solve the food crisis.

10 Nothing has ever stopped scientists from making progress.

1 España tiene la intención de quedarse en la Unión Europea por ahora.

2 Pronto todos compraremos cosas en línea.

3 Sería buena idea comenzar a aprender más sobre informática ahora.

4 Yo que tú no dejaría a mi hijo entrar en esos sitios web libremente.

5 Los avances médicos ayudarán a curar enfermedades de los países en desarrollo.

6 ¿Por qué no pensamos en el daño que vamos a causar al planeta?

7 A todos nos gustaría tener un mundo perfecto.

8 Podría ser fácil pero nadie quiere esforzarse.

9 Sería estupendo que los alimentos transgénicos pudieran resolver la crisis alimentaria.

10 Nada ha impedido jamás que los científicos realicen avances.

Revision of AS Grammar: past tenses – the preterite, imperfect and past continuous

Check the grammar section of Ánimo 2 and/or the Grammar Workbook if you need to know more about any of these areas:

▶ forming and using the preterite tense of regular and irregular verbs: *compré, comí, viví, hice, dije, puse, tuve, fui, estuve, hubo* etc.

▶ radical-changing verbs and when their spelling changes in the preterite tense: *saqué, jugué, empecé, creyó, murió, durmió, pidió, sintió* etc.

▶ forming and using the imperfect tense of regular and irregular verbs: *había, jugaba, comía, vivía, era, veía*

▶ the imperfect tense in time clauses in the past: *hacía cinco años que vivía allí*

▶ when to use the preterite and imperfect tenses: *fue / era, hubo / había*

▶ forming and using the past continuous to show interrupted action: *estaba durmiendo cuando la casa se incendió*

Translate into Spanish

1 How did we live before there were computers?
2 We would listen to the radio and chat to each other.
3 My grandmother used to go shopping nearly every day.
4 She even used to make her own bread if she had time.
5 We had lived in that house for seven years when Grandad died.
6 We were polluting the planet even then, all those years ago.
7 Coal-fired power stations made so much dirty smoke.
8 What were you doing when the first man landed on the moon?
9 A lot of people didn't believe what was happening.
10 Later everyone asked lots of questions about it.

10 Más tarde todos hicieron muchas preguntas acerca de eso.
9 Mucha gente no creyó lo que estaba pasando.
8 ¿Qué estabas haciendo cuando aterrizó el primer hombre en la luna?
7 Las centrales de carbón produjeron mucho humo sucio.
6 Aun entonces, hace muchos años, estábamos contaminando el planeta.
5 Hacía siete años que vivíamos en esa casa cuando murió el abuelo.
4 Hasta hacía su propio pan si tenía tiempo.
3 Mi abuela solía hacer las compras casi todos los días.
2 Escuchábamos la radio y charlábamos.
1 ¿Cómo vivíamos antes de que existieran los ordenadores?

Revision of AS Grammar: compound tenses in the past

:::
Check the grammar section of Ánimo 2 and/or the Grammar Workbook if you need to know more about any of these areas:
:::

▶ forming and using the perfect tense of regular verbs and all irregular past participles: *he, has, ha, hemos, habéis, han jugado / comido / vivido / escrito / dicho / puesto*

▶ forming and using reflexive verbs in the perfect tense: *se ha levantado tarde; ¿a qué hora te has acostado anoche?*

▶ the pluperfect tense: *había jugado; habías comido; habían vivido; había escrito*

▶ the perfect participle: *después de haber hecho esto; habiendo terminado; de haberlo sabido*

Translate into Spanish

1 Before transferring to Barcelona he had played for Sevilla.

2 He had wanted to play for Milan but they wouldn't pay him enough.

3 Having won all three medals there was nothing more to play for.

4 If only we had known this before we arrived.

5 I have written to my teacher again because he hasn't replied to my first letter.

6 After having gone to bed last night I remembered I hadn't put the cat out.

7 How many new states have joined the EU recently?

8 She said she didn't remember what had happened.

9 I would like to have finished it before this weekend.

10 I have never had enough time or money to do half the things I would have liked to do.

que me habría gustado hacer.

10 Nunca he tenido suficiente tiempo ni dinero para hacer ni la mitad de las cosas

9 Me gustaría haberlo terminado antes de este fin de semana.

8 Dijo que no recordaba lo que había pasado.

7 ¿Cuántos estados nuevos se han adherido a la Unión Europea recientemente?

gato.

6 Después de haberme acostado anoche me acordé de que no había sacado al

5 He escrito a mi profesor otra vez porque no ha contestado a mi primera carta.

4 Ojalá lo hubiéramos sabido antes de llegar.

3 Una vez que había ganado las tres medallas, no le quedaba más por lo que jugar.

2 Le hubiera gustado jugar para el Milán, pero no le pagaban lo suficiente.

1 Antes de irse al Barcelona había jugado en el Sevilla.

Revision of AS Grammar: the subjunctive including the imperative forms

The subjunctive mood is used when there are two different clauses in a sentence and the subject of one verb influences the other.

Check the grammar section of Ánimo 2 and/or the Grammar Workbook if you need to know more about any of these areas:

▶ how to form the subjunctive in the present and imperfect tenses

▶ using the subjunctive

▶ after verbs of wanting, requesting and advising: *quiero que hagas esto; me aconsejó que no lo hiciera*

▶ after verbs giving value judgements and expressing emotion: *es una lástima que ...; me sorprende que ...; es increíble que ...*

▶ after verbs expressing doubt or possibility: *dudaba que fuera verdad; puede ser que venga mañana*

▶ after impersonal expressions with adjectives: *es importante que; es imprescindible que ...*

▶ after *cuando* and other expressions of time when referring to the future: *cuando lo sepas dímelo; en cuanto vengas te lo explicaré*

▶ for polite commands – *usted / ustedes* – and **all** negative commands

Translate into Spanish

1 I am happy that my country is part of the European Union.

2 We are angry that the cost of living has gone up so much.

3 It is vital that we teach our children to recycle rubbish.

4 If we go on like this it's possible they won't have a happy future.

5 When they are grown up the world will be a very different place.

6 Please understand that this is not an idle threat.

7 They begged us to respect the environment.

8 Please don't throw your litter all over the mountainside.

9 I am so sorry that they have never appreciated the problem.

10 I have told you so many times not to do that.

10 Te he dicho repetidas veces que no hagas eso.

9 Siento mucho que nunca hayan comprendido el problema.

8 Por favor no arrojen basura por toda la montaña.

7 Nos rogaron que respetáramos el medio ambiente.

6 Por favor comprendan que esto va en serio.

5 Cuando sean mayores el mundo será un lugar muy diferente.

4 Si seguimos así es posible que no tengan un futuro feliz.

3 Es imprescindible que enseñemos a nuestros hijos a reciclar la basura.

2 Nos enfurece que el coste de la vida haya subido tanto.

1 Estoy contento de que mi país sea parte de la Unión Europea.

A2 Grammar: more about the subjunctive

What you need to know

▶ How to form the compound tenses of the subjunctive: *haya vuelto; hubiera querido*

▶ The subjunctive is also used ...

▶ after expressions of purpose: *para que; a fin de que*

▶ after expressions referring to concessions or conditions: *con tal de que; a menos que*

▶ in clauses describing a hypothetical or indefinite noun: *buscamos a una persona que pueda ayudarnos*

▶ in main clauses after
ojalá: ojalá haga sol mañana

tal vez / quizás: quizás vaya a llover más tarde
como si: como si fuera tanto
aunque meaning 'even if ...' but not 'although ...': *aunque fuera a llover*

▶ in set phrases: *sea como sea; digan lo que digan; pase lo que pase*

▶ after words ending in *-quiera* (-ever): *cualquiera, dondequiera*

▶ after *si* when used in past tense clauses which express a sense that the action is impossible or doubtful: *si hiciera esto ...; si lo hubiera sabido*

▶ Don't forget that when you make a sentence negative this often gives it an element of doubt; compare: *Creo que llegarán a tiempo* with *No creo que lleguen a tiempo.*

Translate into Spanish

1 Perhaps we won't ever see an end to terrorism.

2 There will always be a threat to world peace unless we can resolve these conflicts.

3 They doubted that the concert would have raised many funds.

4 I don't think he'll be punished even if he is proven guilty.

5 If only we could find a definite solution to end such poverty.

6 We've been looking for someone to help us sort this problem out.

7 It doesn't matter who so long as they are prepared to work hard.

8 I'm not sure he has enough patience for this type of work.

9 They treated him as if he were a criminal.

10 Wherever you live there will always be some racist attitudes.

1 Tal vez no veamos nunca el fin del terrorismo.

2 Seguirá existiendo una amenaza a la paz mundial a menos que resolvamos estos conflictos.

3 Dudaron que el concierto hubiera recaudado muchos fondos.

4 No creo que sea castigado aunque se le demuestre culpable.

5 Ojalá pudiéramos encontrar una solución definitiva para poner fin a tanta miseria.

6 Hemos estado buscando a alguien que pueda ayudarnos a resolver este problema.

7 No importa quien sea con tal de que esté dispuesto a trabajar duro.

8 No estoy seguro de que tenga suficiente paciencia para este tipo de trabajo.

9 Le trataron como si fuera un criminal.

10 Dondequiera que vivas siempre habrá actitudes racistas.

A2 Grammar: more complex tenses

What you need to know

At A2 Level you are expected to be familiar with the following more complex tenses.

▶ the future perfect:
¡Habré terminado en dos minutos! I will have finished in two minutes!

▶ the conditional perfect:
Habría terminado antes pero no vi la hora. I would have finished sooner but I didn't see the time.

▶ the passive voice in all tenses – don't forget that the past participle must agree:
Tu chaqueta estará terminada el lunes. Your jacket will be finished on Monday.
Ha sido reparada por Juan. It has been repaired by Juan.
Estaba siendo reparada por Miguel. It was being repaired by Miguel.
Fue rota cuando la cojí en un gancho. It was torn when I caught it on a hook.

▶ Don't forget that you can often avoid the passive in Spanish by using either a reflexive form or an active form of the main verb:
Terminaremos tu chaqueta el lunes. We will finish you jacket on Monday.
Juan la ha reparado. Juan has repaired it.
Miguel la estaba reparando. Miguel was repairing it.
La rompí cuando la cojí en un gancho. I tore it when I caught it on a hook.

▶ dependent infinitives, such as *hacer reparar:*
Manda a hacerla reparar. Send it to be repaired / have it repaired.
Hágale entrar. Have him shown in.

Translate into Spanish

1 By 2050 life will have changed a great deal.

2 They will have invented an alternative source of fuel.

3 Will you have recycled everything?

4 She won't have learnt how to use it.

5 You would have liked Almodóvar's latest film.

6 Young criminals would have been locked up years ago.

7 How long will the euro have been in circulation?

8 Can you change this for me?

9 I thought it had already been changed.

10 It was damaged in an accident.

10 Fue dañado en un accidente.

9 Pensé que ya había sido cambiado.

8 ¿Me lo puedes cambiar?

7 ¿Cuánto tiempo habrá estado en circulación el euro?

6 Los delincuentes juveniles habrían sido encarcelados años atrás.

5 Te habría gustado la última película de Almodóvar.

4 No habrá aprendido a usarlo.

3 ¿Habrás reciclado todo?

2 Habrán inventado una fuente alternativa de fuel.

1 De aquí al año 2050 la vida habrá cambiado mucho.

When you are speaking Spanish try to imagine yourself as a Spanish person.

Read aloud to get used to the sound of your own voice in Spanish.

Practise the sounds in front of a mirror – it helps if you can see the way your mouth moves to produce the different sounds.

Record a simple song or an advert and imitate it.

Practise asking questions then answering them yourself.

Beware of reverting to an English accent when you see a word in Spanish which looks like an English word: *televisión* / television.

Make sure you know how to say the alphabet in Spanish in order to spell out words.

The Spanish alphabet: listen to the sounds and repeat them. (Track 4)
A B C D E F G ... H I J K L M ... N Ñ O P Q R ... S T U V W ... X Y Z
It helps to learn them in groups. Sing them to one of your favourite tunes.
Note: *Ññ* is a separate letter in Spanish and comes after *N* in alphabetical lists. All the letters are feminine.

The vowel sounds
Spanish vowels are always clearly pronounced and not relaxed in unstressed syllables as happens in English. **Listen and practise the vowels. (Track 5)**
Alba Arbalaez abre su abanico amarillo amablemente.
Enrique Esquivel escoge el edredón más elegante.
Inés Iglesias indica que es imposible ingresar allí.
Óscar Ordóñez odia las hojas otoñales.
Umberto Umbral usa un uniforme ultramoderno.

Consonants
Spanish *g* is pronounced hard as in 'gate' before *a, o* or *u* and soft like an exaggerated English 'h' before *e* and *i*.
Spanish *c* is pronounced hard as in 'cow' before *a, o* or *u* and soft as in 'thing' before *e* and *i*.

3 Practise these sounds. (Track 6)

hard c: *caballo, conejo, culebra*	**hard g** : *gato, gorila, gusano*
soft c : *cero, cisne*	**soft g** : *gente, gimnasta*

Some spellings change to preserve the sounds:
The hard *c* sound as in 'cow' is written *qu* before *e* or *i*: *sacar* but *saqué*
The hard *g* sound as in 'gate' is written *gu* before *e* or *i*: *pagar* but *pagué*
The soft *c* sound as in 'thing' is written *z* before *a* or *o*: *empecé* but *empezar*
The soft *g* sound like an exaggerated English 'h' is written *j* before *a* or *o*: *coger* but *cojo*
The sound *gu* as in 'guava' is written *gü* before *e* or *i*: *averiguar* but *averigüé*

The position of a consonant in the word also affects its sound: a consonant at the beginning of a word is usually pronounced harder than in the middle or at the end.

La letra d: (Track 7)

donde	*adonde*
dámelo	*me lo ha dado*
drogas	*cuidado*

La letra ll:

llegar	*Sevilla*

La letra r:

revista   pero

La letra s:

sí me gustan las tapas
suelen ser muy malas

La letra x:

exacto   taxi, texto

Try to read out the following tongue-twisters. Compare your pronunciation with the recording. (Track 8)

Es verdad que la ventana verde está en Madrid.
Llora la llama cuando llueve. Que no llore la llama cuando llueva.
Jorge juega ajedrez. Jugando ajedrez Jorge juró jugar con justicia.

r and rr

Listen to the difference between the words *pero* and *perro*. If you have problems with this sound in Spanish, listen and practise it as much as you can. (Track 9)

The letter *r* sounds softer in the middle of a word – *pero, Pedro* – and harder at the beginning of a word: *revista, Roberto*

Double *rr* sounds strongest:
Llora la guitarra con rabia y dulzura.
El perro comió una pera. Pero la perra no comió el peral.

Once you have mastered all the different sounds you need to make sure you are confident about where to place the stress on each word.

Here is the basic rule:

In words which end in a vowel, *s* or *n* the spoken stress falls naturally on the second to last syllable: *instrumento, importantes, representan.*

In words which end in a consonant (except *s* or *n*) the stress falls naturally on the last syllable: *animal, alrededor, nariz.*

All words which do **not** follow this rule require a written accent to indicate where the spoken stress falls: *última, histórico, tecnología.*

Spoken stress and vowels

For the purposes of stress *a*, *e* and *o* are considered to be 'strong' vowels, and *i* and *u* are considered 'weak'.

▶ If the spoken stress falls on a syllable containing two vowels then the stronger one is stressed: *oficial* (pronounced *oficial* not *oficial*).

▶ If both are strong vowels, they are considered to be separate syllables: *levantaos* (pronounced *levantaos*).

▶ If both are weak vowels then the stress falls on the second one: *cuida* (pronounced *cuida* not *cuida*).

▶ If the word does **not** follow these rules then the stress is marked by a written accent: *país, queríamos.*

Finally, having practised all these individual sounds, you need to make sure the whole sentence sounds Spanish.

Intonation (Track 10)

Your voice should rise and fall when you speak.
In Spanish it should fall:

▶ at the end of a short sentence. *Toco la guitarra.* (I play the guitar.)

It should rise:

▶ at the end of another type of question: *¿Tienes una flauta?* (Have you got a flute?)

▶ in the middle of longer sentences:
Tú tienes una flauta y yo tengo una guitarra.
(You've got a flute and I've got a guitar.)

Sinalefa and *entrelazamiento* (Track 11)

In spoken Spanish, vowel sounds and consonants slide into each other, which helps to make the sentence flow.
When vowel sounds end and begin consecutive words they are linked together. This is known as **sinalefa**.
A final consonant is linked together with a following vowel. This is known as **entrelazamiento**.

1 Copy these words and phrases and indicate the *sinalefa* and *entrelazamiento*.

2 Listen to these verses and try to imitate the pronunciation.

El otoño: isla
de perfil estricto
que pone en olvido
la onda indecisa.

¡Amor a la línea!
La vid se desnuda
de una vestidura
demasiado rica.

¡Oh claridad! Pía
tanto entre las hojas
que quieren ser todas
a un tiempo amarillas.

¡Trabazón de brisas
entre cielo y álamo!
Y todo el espacio,
tan continuo, vibra.

Esta luz antigua
de tarde feliz
no puede morir.
¡Ya es mía, ya es mía!

Unit 1 – La energía y la contaminación

la contaminación	*pollution*
generar	*to generate / create*
la calefacción	*heating*
los residuos	*waste*
el vertedero	*rubbish dump*
enterrar	*to submerge / bury*
emitir	*to emit / give off*
verter	*to spill / pour away*
la sequía	*drought*
la desertificación	*desertification*
químico/a	*chemical*
escalofriante	*staggering / mind-blowing*
la energía eólica	*wind energy*
los aerogeneradores	*wind turbines*
las hélices	*turbines / propellers*
fotovoltaico/a	*solar*
invernadero	*greenhouse*
un derroche	*a waste*
el calentamiento global	*global warming*
costear el lujo	*to afford*
empeñarse en	*to be determined*
atascado/a	*blocked up*
concienciar	*to make aware*
la desaceleración	*slowing down*
contundente	*overwhelming*
el auge	*boom*
el desplome	*nosedive*
frenar	*to brake / put a stop to*
incrementar	*to increase*
rechazar	*to reject*
inocuo/a	*harmless*
dañino/a	*harmful*
el riesgo	*risk*
agotar	*to run out of*
la huella de carbono	*carbon footprint*
vedar	*to ban, prohibit*

Unit 2 – ¡SOS Protejamos nuestro planeta!

el entorno	*surroundings / environs*
transgénico/a	*GM (crops)*
amenazar	*to threaten*
la cadena	*chain*
la deforestación	*deforestation*
el propósito	*purpose / reason*
desperdiciar	*to waste*
aprovechar	*to take advantage of / maximise*
las materias primas	*raw materials*
la degradación	*spoiling / decomposition*
las latas	*tins*
envases tipo brick	*cartons*
vidrio	*glass*
provisto	*provided*
el veredicto	*verdict*
quejarse	*to complain*
abordar	*to tackle / deal with*
sensato/a	*sensible*
el desplazamiento	*displacement*
las emisiones	*exhaust*
medio	*average*
un ahorro	*a saving*
yendo a	*going to*
apoyar	*to support*
el impacto paisajístico	*impact on the countryside*
las vías ferroviarias	*railways*
el deterioro	*deterioration*
caber	*to fit in*
el crecimiento	*increase*
desmesurado/a	*enormous / excessive*
los umbrales	*threshold*
la alfabetización	*literacy*
cotidiano/a	*daily*
abastecer	*to provide*
nocivo/a	*harmful*

Unit 3 – Tierras cosmopólitas

acoger	*to welcome*
de acogida	*reception*
el rechazo	*rejection*
prejuicio	*prejudice*
la convivencia	*coexistence*
el asilo	*asylum*
la inmigración	*immigration*
huir	*to flee*
la incertidumbre	*uncertainty*
adinerado/a	*wealthy*
sobrevivir	*to survive*
la osadía	*daring*
intentar	*to attempt to*
imprevisto/a	*unforeseen*
el fracaso	*failure*
la plantilla laboral	*workforce*
la vivienda	*housing*
el matadero	*slaughterhouse*
mezclarse	*to mix*
atraer	*to attract*
alquilar	*to hire*
el gueto	*ghetto*
desacato/a	*contempt / disobeying*
ajustar	*to adjust*
salvaguardar	*to safeguard*
una patera	*raft*
forastero/a	*foreign*
carecer de	*to lack*
brindar	*to offer*
el capataz	*foreman*
la discapacidad	*disability*
las chabolas	*shanty town / shacks*
aguantar	*to put up with*
encarcelar	*to imprison*
un temporero	*temporary worker*
denunciar	*to denounce*
empadronar	*to register (with authorities)*

Unit 4 – La riqueza y la pobreza

la riqueza	*wealth*
la pobreza	*poverty*
prestigioso/a	*famous / renowned*
el terreno	*land*
el ingreso	*income*
el sueldo medio	*average wage*
un tercio	*a third*
la tasa de	*rate of*
enriquecerse	*to get rich*
empobrecerse	*to become poor*
el comercio libre	*free trade*
el consumismo	*consumerism*
las tarifas	*taxes / tariffs*
los subsidios	*subsidies*
un dineral	*a vast amount of money*
dar de comer a	*to feed*
el microcrédito	*microcredit*
invertir	*to invest*
prestar	*to lend*
criar	*to rear*
la cabra	*goat*
conllevar	*to bring with*
pudiendo	*being able to*
el presupuesto	*budget*
mudo/a	*dumb*
divergente	*opposite*
mejorar	*to make better*
sin afán de lucro	*without interest*
fomentar	*to encourage*
un diputado	*a member of parliament*
desafiar	*to challenge*
las subvenciones	*subsidies*
la empresa	*company*
superarse	*to improve oneself*

Unit 5 – El crimen y el castigo

el castigo	*punishment*
el delito	*offence / crime*
las pandillas	*gangs*
la cárcel	*prison*
el recluso	*prisoner*
la fianza	*bail*
culpable	*guilty*
un abogado	*a lawyer*
la ciencia forense	*forensic science*
una anciana	*an old lady*
en el punto de mira	*(to have) in one's sights / one's eyes on*
vinculado/a	*linked to*
reprimir	*to repress*
la riña	*brawl / fight*
equivocado/a	*mistaken*
la red	*a network*
apoyar	*to help / back up*
aliarse	*to get together*
luchar	*to struggle / fight*
el lastre	*burden / might / full force*
el malhechor	*evildoer / wicked person*
una celda	*a cell*
aliviarse	*to alleviate / make better*
el narcotraficante	*drugs trafficker*
despreciar	*to despise*
las pautas	*guidelines / criteria*
alegar	*to allege*
tramitar	*to deal with*
comparecer ante	*to appear before / be judged by*
las cortes	*court*
atracar	*to assault / mug*
el desempleo	*unemployment*
los derechos	*rights*
detener	*to detain*

Unit 6 – Avances científicos, médicos y tecnológicos

los avances	*advances*
la clonación	*cloning*
el ADN	*DNA*
los OGM	*GMO's*
la nanotecnología	*nanotechnology*
la reproducción asistida	*IVF*
las prótesis	*prosthetics*
el ordenador	*computer*
el portal	*webpage / portal*
el ratón	*mouse*
potente	*powerful*
capaz de	*capable of*
la cirugía	*surgery*
el tejido	*tissue*
indeseado/a	*undesirable*
el tamaño	*size*
afrontar	*to confront / face up to*
sobrepesar	*to outweigh*
discapacitado/a	*disabled*
el trasplante	*transplant*
una célula	*a cell*
el rechazo	*rejection*
la escasez	*scarcity*
descubrir	*to discover*
el descubrimiento	*discovery*
la compra en línea	*online shopping*
el desarrollo	*development*
la carrera espacial	*space race*
las misiones espaciales	*space missions*
el artilugio	*artefact / gadget*
puntero/a	*at the forefront*
ingenioso/a	*ingenious / clever*
el dispositivo	*gadget*
una sonda	*space probe*
el hallazgo	*finding / discovery*
respaldar	*to back up*
una herramienta	*tool*
los internautas	*Internet users*

Unit 7 – Talento hispano

los artes	*arts*
las artes visuales	*visual arts*
la escultura	*sculpture*
la lengua	*language / tongue*
ambientarse	*to take place*
pretender	*to try to*
la meta	*aim*
la palabra escrita	*written word*
las dotes	*gifts / talents*
una afición	*a hobby*
el estreno	*debut / first showing / premier*
el espectador	*spectator*
sorprender	*to surprise*
destacar	*to stand out*
hacer burla de	*to make fun of*
entretenido/a	*entertaining*
desconcertante	*disconcerting / upsetting*
la pantalla	*screen*
la rebeldía	*rebelliousness*
los modales	*manners*
el orfanato	*orphanage*
arrasar	*to take by storm*
pegadizo/a	*catchy*
sin pudor	*no decency*
escandalizarse	*to scandalise*
enfurecerse	*to make furious*
un espectáculo	*a show*
las palmas	*palms (of hand)*
los tacones	*heels (of shoe)*
el remordimiento	*remorse*
el destino	*destiny*
arrepentirse	*to repent*

Unit 8 – Patrimonio e historia

el patrimonio	*heritage*
el auge	*rise*
el ocaso	*fall*
el crisol	*melting pot*
las tinieblas	*dark ages*
la fe	*faith / religion*
asolar	*to lay waste / ravage*
la dictadura	*dictatorship*
la derrota	*defeat*
lograr	*to succeed in*
desvanecer	*to fade*
indígenos	*native*
los inmigrantes	*immigrants*
independizarse	*to become independent*
el apodo	*nickname*
bilingüe	*bilingual*
gratis	*for free*
agradecido/a	*thankful*
una nueva ola	*a new wave*
la población	*population*
la plata	*silver*
el estaño	*tin*
la lucha	*struggle*
cruento/a	*bloody*
los hitos	*milestones / landmarks*
la cámera	*chamber (as in government)*
el sindicato	*union of workers*
aprobar	*to approve / pass a law*
una herida	*wound*
el rehén	*hostage*
adolorido/a	*upset / hurt*
la soberanía	*sovereignty*
entregarse	*to hand over / give in*
borrar	*to rub out / erase*
la tasa de natalidad	*birthrate*

Unit 9 – Política y polémicas globales

gobernar / el gobierno	*to govern / government*
la hambruna	*famine / hunger*
la deuda	*debt*
las pandemias	*pandemics*
acercar	*to approach / draw near*
la desigualdad	*inequality*
audaz	*daring*
innegable	*undeniable*
dictaminar	*to dictate*
autogobierno	*self-rule*
los arquetipos	*stereotypes*
el colmo	*limit*
respaldar	*to back up*
la mili	*military service*
la botellona	*binge drinking*
culpar	*to blame*
un juicio	*a trial*
un régimen	*a regime (government)*
un intercambio	*an exchange*
radicar	*to have roots*
el comportamiento	*behaviour*
el poder	*power*
el lema	*slogan*
manifestar	*to protest*
la campaña	*campaign*
apelar	*to appeal to*
los asesinos	*assassins*
disfrazarse	*to disguise oneself*
matar / la matanza	*to kill / killing*
dispares	*disparate*
alcanzar	*to achieve / reach*
fracasar / un fracaso	*to fail / failure*
amenazar	*to threaten*
entrometerse	*to meddle*
un juez	*a judge*

Translation task 1

a) Tras meses de muy poca lluvia Cataluña ha tenido que pedir ayuda a Madrid.

b) Sin embargo es dudoso que puedan resolver el problema rápidamente.

c) El país está luchando por resolver la peor sequía en cuarenta años.

d) Cataluña, en el noreste, ha sido gravemente afectada.

e) Las autoridades de Barcelona van a multar a la gente por regar el jardín.

f) No se permite a nadie llenar una piscina de más de 300 metros cuadrados.

g) Las fuentes han sido vaciadas y las duchas de la playa cerradas.

Translation task 2

Suggested translation

Hoy en día todos somos muy conscientes de los aspectos positivos del Internet y somos pocos los que no nos aprovechamos de ellos. Nadie duda que sea una herramienta poderosa que trae enormes beneficios a sus usuarios. Además, los precios están bajando cada día más, de modo que es cada vez más accesible para un mayor número de personas.

Sin embargo, al mismo tiempo es importante reconocer que el Internet es un foro público y por consiguiente se presta al abuso. Como consecuencia todos debemos cuidarnos de la clase de información que damos por Internet, pero sobre todo debemos insistir en que el gobierno desarrolle leyes para combatir los delitos cibernéticos y ayude a proteger los usuarios menores de edad.

infinitive	present	preterite	imperfect	future	conditional	present subjunctive	imperfect subjunctive	present participle	past participle
comprar	compro	compré	compraba	compraré	compraría	compre	comprara/se	comprando	comprado
to buy	I buy	I bought	I used to buy	I will buy	I would buy	buy	bought	buying	bought
comer	como	comí	comía	comeré	comería	coma	comiera/se	comiendo	comido
subir	subo	subí	subía	subiré	subiría	suba	subiera/se	subiendo	subido
levantarse	me levanto	me levanté	me levantaba	me levantaré	me levantaría	me levante	me levantara/se	levantándome	levantado
dar	doy	di	daba	daré	daría	dé	diera/se	dando	dado
decir	digo	dije	decía	diré	diría	diga	dijera/se	diciendo	dicho
estar	estoy	estuve	estaba	estaré	estaría	esté	estuviera/se	estando	estado
haber	he	hube	había	habré	habría	haya	hubiera/se	habiendo	habido
hacer	hago	hice	hacía	haré	haría	haga	hiciera/se	haciendo	hecho
ir	voy	fui	iba	iré	iría	vaya	fuera/se	yendo	ido
poder	puedo	pude	podía	podré	podría	pueda	pudiera/se	pudiendo	podido
poner	pongo	puse	ponía	pondré	pondría	ponga	pusiera/se	poniendo	puesto
querer	quiero	quise	quería	querré	querría	quiera	quisiera/se	queriendo	querido
saber	sé	supe	sabía	sabré	sabría	sepa	supiera/se	sabiendo	sabido
ser	soy	fui	era	seré	sería	sea	fuera/se	siendo	sido
tener	tengo	tuve	tenía	tendré	tendría	tenga	tuviera/se	teniendo	tenido
traer	traigo	traje	traía	traeré	traería	traiga	trajera/se	trayendo	traído
venir	vengo	vine	venía	vendré	vendría	venga	viniera/se	viniendo	venido